FRIDA KAHLO

The Lonely Artist

THE HISTORY HOUR

HISTORY

CONTENTS

❧ I ❧

INTRODUCTION

❦

Frida Kahlo was in and of herself an enigma to many that followed her work over the years and as with most painters and singers, her work is worth more since she has passed away than what it was worth during her life.

❦

Frida was ahead of her time. She was bisexual and would have fit in perfectly in the time we live in now. She would be a real hit in the LGBTQ community and fit right in with them.

❦

Her disabilities would be acceptable in our society of today and her husband, Diego would probably be run out of town by the Real Housewives of "***Cheaters***."

⚜

I am afraid that her unibrow, mustache, and underarm hair may not go over but what do I know?

⚜

Frida came with a lot of baggage in her life starting when she was only six years old and even more baggage piled on when she was in high school. Her suffering was more than anyone can imagine but she kept her head held high and forged her way forward.

⚜

It remains a mystery as to how someone with her looks, someone not attractive in any form or fashion and with all her deformities, that she was able to attract so many rich, famous and handsome men and hold them under her spell.

⚜

At the same time, her husband Diego weighing in at 300 pounds, bulging eyes, and rotting teeth could have any woman he wiggled his finger toward.

⚜

How does this happen?

⚜

Please read this book and tell me if you can figure out how you think the two of them could attract the opposite sex. I am still curious after all my research!

❧ II ❧
FRIDA'S BIRTH AND
FAMILY

"I was a child who went about in a world of colors...
My friends, my companions, became women slowly; I
became old in instants."

— FRIDA KAHLO

❧

Magdalena Carmen Frieda Kahlo came into this world July 6,
1907, and later changed her name to Frida Kahlo in Coyoacan, Mexico City, Mexico. According to an official birth
registry, her birth was in her maternal grandmother's home
who lived nearby.

❧

Frida's father was born Carl Wilhelm Kahlo but later changed it to Guillermo Kahlo. Frida tried to tell everyone he was of the Jewish-Hungarian bloodline, but when you follow his ancestry, it is a fact that his genealogy shows he was a German. He was born in Pforzheim, of Baden, Germany. His father was a jeweler Jakob Heinrich Kahlo and his mother was Henriette Kaufmann. His parents were Lutheran.

❦

His photography seemed to be in a constant request as he documented with his photos important churches, industries, companies, architectural works, street landmarks that allowed his work to be of documental and historical significance in Mexico at the dawn of the 20th century.

❦

Frida's father attended college at Germany's University of Nuremberg. Since he could not get along with his stepmother, his father paid him to move to Mexico in 1891. When he moved to Mexico in July of 1894, he sought citizenship there.

❦

Kahlo had married Maria Cardena in late 1893, and she gave him three children. The night of their third child's birth, Maria died during the birth process. Kahlo wasted no time and asked Antonio Calderon that same night if he could marry his daughter Matilde. Once they married, he sent the children that had belonged to him and Maria to a convent to grow up.

❦

Frida was born to her mestiza (Spanish/American India mother, Matilde, and her Guillermo, the photographer who had come to Mexico where he met her mother and they married.

※

No one knew why Matilde was hesitant to breastfeed Frida, but Matilde quickly handed Frida off to two Indian women to act as wet nurses. The first wet nurse was fired per Matilde because of the Indian woman's drinking.

※

It may have been because of all the confusion, maybe having erratic caregivers' times three, and Matilde's losing her son that Frida called the environment of their household "*sad*." Possibly from early childhood on Frida had a lowered sense of self-esteem.

※

Kahlo's father set up his photography studio in 1901, working for an El Mundo and Seminario Ilustrado. The Mexican government commissioned him to take architectural photos, which would probably be some of his best work.

※

Frida usually gave her date of birth as July 7th, 1910, a fundamental lie for Frida. It makes her three years younger than what she truly was when she was born in 1907.

※

father, Guillermo who had epilepsy, but not so
ther, Matilde. After Frida, there was another
eleven months later, Cristina. Before Frida's
a son who only lived a few days after he
arrived in this world.

ಚಿತ್ರ

Frida had three sisters, Cristina, Adriana, and Matilde. She also had two half-sisters from her father's first marriage, Margarita and Maria Luisa but they lived at a Catholic School.

ಚಿತ್ರ

When Frida was about six years old, she developed polio, but her parents did not pick up on the fact early enough that she was ill. When her leg started to wither and get thin, her parents thought it had been caused by "*that little boy who had thrown a wood log at her foot.*"

ಚಿತ್ರ

Frida became bedridden for about nine months. She recovered from polio, but still had a limp whenever she walked as polio had made her leg thin and her foot became stunted in growth.

ಚಿತ್ರ

Frida kept trying to hide her withered leg by wrapping it with bandages, so it would look larger, and then wear thick wool socks so her foot would not be noticeable. As Frida grew, she never wore a leg brace nor an orthopedic shoe which may have changed the course of her deformities.

Because of her withered leg causing her limp, it caused her spinal column and pelvis to deform and twist as she grew according to one physician. It is argued by another physician who recently stated that his diagnosis for her would be that she had spina bifida, a congenital condition. One doctor feels that this could have been part of her problem with childbearing.

While she would be recovering, her Dad was the one who kept her active by having her swim, play soccer, and at times wrestle which was a different sport for a little girl at that time in history, but her Dad would do anything to help her recover. She grew up with a deformity of one leg shorter than the other, and this caused her to be bullied by the other children.

Her father helped her learn photography, and she started helping him develop, retouch and color photographs. She took up roller skating, bicycling, wrestling, boxing, and swimming despite the fact they were mostly sports for boys.

When Frida got older, she described her home life as a child as one that was usually "***very, very sad***." It seemed her parents were both sick all the time and she could sense that her parents did not love each other making her feel constantly uneasy.

⚜

Frida states that her mother and father did spoil her a lot and loved her more than her other sisters. Some feel that statement, in all its despair, does provide the sad key to Frida's psyche.

⚜

For the remainder of her life, Frida would always associate pain with love and attention. She would through her entire life use sickness to get the attention that she craved so desperately from others.

⚜

It is easy to see during her adolescent years in family photographs that she used this unusual method to get attention and the entire time she would disguise her withered leg.

⚜

All her relatives around her in the pictures were dressed in their good clothes while Frida would be wearing some natty masculine three-piece suit with a necktie as she cross-dressed. The early cross-dressing could also point to a problem with her having a young gender identity.

⚜

Frida felt that the most important parts of her body were her unibrow, her eyes, and her brain. Other than that, she did not like anything about her body. She said her genitals and breasts were only average, her head too small, and felt that she was like the opposite sex in that she always had a mustache.

Frida felt her mother was an

"intelligent, active, and kind person, but was also cruel, a religious fanatic, and constantly calculating."

৬৩৫৪৩

Frida's father's photography business suffered terribly during the Mexican Revolution of 1910-1920, even though the overthrown government commissioned photography work from him, but the Revolution that dragged on for ten years kept his private paying clients away.

৬৩৫৪৩

No matter how much Frida tried to hide her deformity by wearing long skirts, pants and doubling on the number of socks she wore, it was still evident by the limp that she had that handicapped her.

৬৩৫৪৩

When you look at Frida's medical records, they are so vague it is hard to decide if she had polio or another condition at that time the medical community called "***white tumor***."

৬৩৫৪৩

Because of polio, Frida started school later than peers her age. In the beginning, along with her sister Cristina, they went to the local kindergarten and then primary school and their parents felt they would be better off for the fifth and sixth grades to be homeschooled.

◌⁜◌

Frida then enrolled in a German school and earned the name of '**Peg Leg Frida**,' and where Sara Zenil, her teacher for anatomy and gym had noticed the condition of Frida's leg.

◌⁜◌

Zenil said that Frida was too fragile and pulled her out of the sports program and began a '**physical relationship**' with Frida. It was Frida's first sexual experience, at the age of thirteen years. Frida's mother found some letters between Zenil and Frida and immediately removed Frida from the German school and placed her in the National Preparatory School instead. Frida was one of the 35 girls out of 2,000 students.

◌⁜◌

The National Preparatory School was a very elite institution in 1922. Frida wanted to focus on sciences and then go to medical school.

◌⁜◌

While she was at the National Preparatory School, she became involved with a group that was rebelling against anything that looked or sounded conservative. It was here at this time she joined the Young Communist League and the Mexican Communist Party.

❧

Everyone came to know Frida for her seemingly happy spirit and her brightly colored jewelry and clothes.

❧

Frida kept a lot of notes and diaries that helped you better to see into her life as the daughter of a Catholic Indian-Spanish mother given to hysterics and a lower-middle-class Jewish-German father photographer that caused Frida to turn into a famous, celebrated painter.

❧

Frida seemed to be a promiscuous charmer, a communist, and then during her diary years, she became a dykish, narcotic addicted, amputee who was suicidal and afflicted with Munchausen syndrome (someone who likes being sick for the attention it will get them.)

❧

Since her mother and father could never have a son, Frida felt it her responsibility to take on the role of a son for the family. She was her dad's favorite, and always the one who could identify with him the best.

❧

In 1932 Frida and one of her good friends made a trip to Mexico because Frida's mother was ill. On September 15th, Frida's mother died unexpectedly at 56 years old. She had breast cancer, but two days before her death she had gone through a simple gallbladder surgery where they removed 160 gallstones.

⚶

Frida's mother Matilde Calderon De Kahlo died from gallstones and breast cancer. Different publications indicate that Frida became inconsolable when her mother died. It makes one question if the relationship Frida had with her mother was strained, or if it was more likely a bond between a passionate, headstrong daughter and a determined, practical mother.

⚶

What made this trip unusual was that they said Frida never went to see her mother. She only went to Mexico, but never visited her mother.

⚶

April 14th, 1941 Frida's father dies of what some say was a heart attack, while there are others who feel it was his epilepsy during a seizure. We now know there are more and more deaths happening during epileptic seizures than ever. Before and during an autopsy, they cannot find any answer as to why the seizure caused the death.

⚶

Frida was devastated as she loved her father so much. He loved her deeply, and she knew it. It was about this time that Frida had to have treatments for syphilis. Frida went into a deep depression after losing her Dad.

❧ III ❧
FRIDA AND DIEGO BEGIN
THEIR LIFE TOGETHER

"I love you more than my own skin."

— FRIDA KAHLO

༺❁༻

1925 changed Frida's life again forever. She was now an apprentice and sleeping with an artist friend of her dad's. They were riding a school bus when a wooden trolley car hit their bus broadside.

༺❁༻

The wooden trolley blew up into a thousand pieces. Frida became skewered with the metal handrail of the trolley that entered in the lower part of her body on her left side and came out through her vagina, tearing the left lip (labia) of her vagina.

❧

The accident broke her pelvis and spinal column in three places along with the breaking of two ribs and her collarbone. Her withered leg shattered, eleven fractures in it alone, her right foot was crushed and dislocated.

❧

During the impact, all of Frida's clothes had been knocked off, and she was laying there in the public nude. What was weirder, there was someone on the bus who had to be carrying a pack of gold powder. Strange as it may seem, the package broke, the gold spilled out and fell all over the Frida's bleeding body, making her glisten in gold. Frida had to stay in the hospital for a month.

❧

Because of some of their mutual Communist friends, Frida met Diego Rivera. They soon began an affair after Frida showed up where he was working one day and demanded the look at her paintings and critique what she had painted.

❧

Rivera and Frida married in 1929, and it seemed doomed from the start to all those who knew both of them. Diego was twenty-one years older than Frida, he was taller than six feet, and 200 pounds heavier than Frida. He was as irresistible as much as he was ugly. Frida said he looked like a *"boy frog standing on his hind legs."*

It is hard to understand why women threw themselves at him. Famous women swooned around him all the time.

⊗⊗⊗

He was casual with his unfaithfulness and did not care if Frida found out and at the same time it was like a compulsion with him. Diego was almost narcissistic when it came to women and what he desired to make himself happy at the expense of others.

⊗⊗⊗

Diego was repulsive when he compared urinating to making love and told everyone he could be a lesbian since he loved women so much.

⊗⊗⊗

Frida was crazy about him, and she talked about him constantly in the diaries she wrote. She even loved his massive stomach as she describes it to be tight and like a smooth sphere and that his breast was so sensitive and large.

⊗⊗⊗

Frida seemed to alter her personality to please her new husband. She began dressing in feminine costumes of the Tehuantepec, wearing her hair in Indian styles and even using different painting techniques.

⊗⊗⊗

Frida turned up pregnant right before they were married but lost the baby at three months. The reason for the loss was supposedly due to her twisted pelvis. She became pregnant again, and it also ended in a miscarriage, but this time she tried to provoke the abortion by swallowing quinine.

❦

The third pregnancy also resulted in an abortion, but this may have been due to it being one of her lover's children. No one knows for sure, but this may have also been provoked.

❦

Most think that Frida not bringing a child to term is pure myth. Especially the last two '*miscarriages*' if you want to call them that. It seems she did not want children; they would have gotten in her way with all the lovers she had both male and female.

❦

It does seem strange with her ovaries being so underdeveloped congenitally that she was even able to conceive. With her knowing that her pelvis was so damaged as it was by the terrible bus accident it makes one wonder why she would never think about trying to bear a child to full term.

❦

Diego said that he worried if she had a child, it would worsen her health as it was so delicate. Others say that if she could physically carry a child, psychologically she would never be able to as it would get in the way with her bond to Diego.

She babied Diego so much that she would fill his tub full of children's toys as she bathed him. Frida would travel with Diego when he went to New York, Detroit, and San Francisco during the time he worked for American industrialists for large commissions by painting leftist themes.

In the late 1930's Frida visited the home of Edgar and Liliane Kaufmann at Fallingwater; the house designed by Frank Loyd Wright. Much controversy swirls around the house today as Wright designed the house in under three hours and the design of the house hangs out over the falls and is tipping towards falling from the cliff.

The story of that night goes that Julian Levy and Edgar Kaufmann were competing for Frida's affections all night long, but she had come with Julian Levy, and Levy won the night with Frida.

Frida practiced her painting, made some crucial contacts in the art and social world. It ran from the Rockefellers all the way to Louise Nevelson (who everyone feels was one of Diego's conquests).

It seemed the entire time that Diego and Frida were in New

York during 1933 and worked for Nelson Rockefeller at the RCA Building there was nothing but controversy. Rockefeller stopped Diego from going any further on the mural he was painting for him because Diego insisted on placing a portrait of Vladimir Lenin, a communist leader into the mural. Rockefeller made sure the painting was covered never to be in the view of the public in the future. Months after the incident, Frida and Diego returned to Mexico and decided to live in San Angel.

◈

Frida got smart in her techniques however and changed her tactics with Diego's mistresses. She would disarm them by becoming their best friend and at times it would turn into a physical relationship.

◈

Frida got homesick while she was in the United States, so she talked Diego who was reluctant to do so, to go back to Mexico. They did go back, but he was vindictive about it and had an affair with Frida's sister Cristina.

❧ IV ❧
DIEGO'S FIRST FIGHT
WITH PENILE CANCER

"I never paint dreams or nightmares. I paint my own reality."

— FRIDA KAHLO

❧

Diego, in the long run, did pay a price of sorts for his continuous priapism; in the 1960s he developed cancer of his penis.

❧

Diego, who had more sexual partners than even he could have counted over the years had grown up and lived in a country where they did not practice circumcision and was ultimately diagnosed with penile cancer.

❧

Diego said he first noticed that he was having pain in the region of his penis and it was swelling and he could not urinate. He saw his doctor, and they ran the usual tests, but the diagnosis was not what Diego was expecting when they told him he had cancer.

❧

He absolutely would not allow them to remove his penis surgically (penectomy) and testicles to prevent cancer from spreading and instead of surgery since he was a Communist, he traveled to the Soviet Union to have radiation therapy. They were not treating with cobalt treatments, or some called it radiation therapy in Mexico or the United States at that time.

❧

Diego could not begin to think about giving up the organs of his body that had given him the most pleasure of his life.

❧

After undergoing a few months of the '*x-ray therapy treatments*,' which were '*cobalt*' treatments at the time, Diego's symptoms disappeared. His doctor in the Soviet Union ran another biopsy, and it confirmed the malignancy was no longer spreading. It is important to notice that the malignancy was arrested; they did not tell Diego he was cured. It was in remission, but Diego did not understand that concept and felt he had an amazing recovery.

※

Since this scared Diego so much, he changed his diet so that he ate much healthier. His doctor had told him that for every two pounds he lost, he would live another year.

※

Diego describes that when he was going through his treatments that he suffered a deep depression that was personal. Diego said he felt like his life was over.

※

During treatment and while painting a mural at a new hospital Diego was hit by a painful notion that flashed through his mind. He was looking at his painting when he realized that physical love was over for him and that he was now an old man. He was too sick and too old even to be able to enjoy the ecstasy of making love.

❧ V ❧

FRIDA'S LOVERS

"Feet, what do I need you for when I have wings to fly?"

— FRIDA KAHLO

❧

Frida was devastated and started painting herself as bleeding and wounded. It seems that from Frida's diaries that when she started her revenge extramarital affairs, it was after Diego cheated on her with her sister Cristina.

❧

Frida did whatever she could to keep Diego from finding out about her heterosexual trysts. It wasn't as difficult when they moved into their '**his-and-hers**' houses that were connected by a bridge after their second wedding.

※

When Diego would find out about Frida's male indiscretions, they would usually stop even though he was never faithful. Little did he know that Frida was quietly keeping tabs on Diego as well.

※

Nickolas Muray was not born as Nickolas Muray but Miklos Mandl in Hungary. His name you will find in the Birth Register of the Jewish Community, but he did not have a Jewish name.

※

Samu, his father, two years later, who was a postal employee, packed up their family and moved them to Budapest so his children could get a better education and they may have a chance at more job prospects.

※

Nickolas was his parents favorite because he was unusually handsome, the most intelligent, and had a charming personality. The flip side of the coin, said he was strong-willed, had a temper, could not handle the word '**no**' for an answer, and he was rebellious.

※

It seemed he was humiliated over and over by the rampant anti-Semitism, he still hated being denied for being Jewish when he wasn't, and it seemed the opportunities were given to other boys.

⚜

Because of this Nickolas decided as a boy that one day he was going to see the world, and not be confined to the impositions by an unfair society.

⚜

Nickolas Muray may have been born in Hungary but became an American photographer and even an Olympic fencer. Nickolas went on to Budapest for graphic arts school and studied photoengraving, photography, and lithography.

⚜

In 1913 the threat of war was looming in Europe, so Murray took off for New York. It was in 1923 that Nickolas Murray ran into artist Miguel Covarrubias and the friendship would forever change Nick's life. The two of them sold photographs to some of the same magazines and other publications, and they became best friends.

⚜

He was soon recognized as a great portrait photographer. It so happened that his subjects were mostly New York celebrities. In 1929 he was hired to start photographing the movie stars of Hollywood.

On one such occasion, Nickolas visited Miguel in his home country of Mexico in 1931. During that one trip, Nickolas and Frida met, but she and Diego were still married. One thing is for sure their meeting at that time was convenient for them because Frida was supposed to be with Diego in San Francisco.

Nickolas and Frida started an on again and off again affair that lasted ten years. It outlasted Nickolas's third marriage to a Monica O'Shea, his second wife that he had married in 1930. She told him in the year 1937 that she was leaving and divorcing him on the grounds of cruelty.

Nickolas and Frida's affair would last over a decade, and they would travel to be with each other in New York and Mexico. Correspondence between the two of them is rich about their love affair and with Nick's many portraits he made of Frida.

Frida divorced Diego in 1939 and Muray had his hopes that Frida would then marry him. Frida soon let his hopes down when she turned around and remarried Diego again the very next year.

Muray wanted to marry Frida, but it did become apparent

after all the years that Frida only wanted Muray as a lover, not as her husband. At this point, Muray left for good and took his fourth wife, Peggy. He stayed friends with Frida until she died.

ॐ

Nickolas Muray died in 1965 during a fencing match in New York City from a massive heart attack.

ॐ

Diego with his macho beliefs felt it was okay that he could be unfaithful whenever he desired and had numerous extramarital affairs.

ॐ

Frida had affairs with so many men and women. Most of the women she had sexual trysts with were merely to get even with Diego for some reason or other.

ॐ

During 1936 (remember she was still involved in an affair with Nick Muray) Frida had a fling with Isamu Noguchi, a Japanese-American sculptor. Isamu was in bed with Frida when one of her servants, a houseboy, came to her and said that Diego was on his way there.

ॐ

Isamu hopped out of Frida's bed, grabbed his clothes, shimmied down a tree that was growing next to the patio and made his narrow escape over their roof just in time.

❦

There was still a problem however that neither Isamu nor Frida knew about and that was one of Frida's hairless dogs had gotten hold of one of Isamu's socks and carried it off and who do you think found it? Of course, it was Diego that saw the incriminating piece of evidence. When Diego and Isamu crossed paths again, Diego told Isamu that he was going to shoot him.

❦

Isamu being an introvert and tranquil person who just wanted to live in the world unnoticed, was still a famous person due to his charming, brilliant, but physical beauty, and the ability to seduce women. Isamu kept his private life private and would at times seclude himself from the world.

❦

In the world Isamu lived in, he felt that a child's space should be just as valuable as that of an adult. He was famous for designing beautiful and experimental play spots for children that could be more fun than a swing set or a slide.

❦

Although Frida and Isamu had been found out about by Diego, they too remained friends for the rest of their natural lives.

※

But, just as crazy was when Diego would brag to anyone that would listen about the stories of Frida's sexual flings and the women she would choose to involve.

※

The one male partner that Frida had that made Diego the angriest was Leon Trotsky that Diego himself had used his political pull to bring to Mexico in 1937. (Here again, Frida was still very involved with Nick Muray.)

※

Leon Trotsky exiled from his own country at 58 years old, along with his wife Natalia Sedova made it to Tampico, Mexico on a Norwegian oil tanker that was heavily guarded on January 9th, 1937.

※

At the time of their arrival, Diego was in the hospital with eye and kidney problems and could not make it to the port to greet them. Diego sent Frida to meet them who was there with journalists, government officials, and Communist Party members. Frida went back with them to Coyoacan, and her home with Diego at La Casa Azul, where the Trotskys would live with heavy protection and every wish they desired met for two years.

※

Frida was still mad, hurt and angry from learning that Diego had an affair with her little sister, Cristina. To get even Frida took quick advantage and openly flirted with Trotsky, who must have been thinking he had gone to heaven with all this attention from such a young woman. That spring the emotional affair they shared grew into a physical one.

❦

Some of their trysts took place at Frida's sister, Cristina's house, which Diego was the one who probably bought for her, along with the furnishings of red leather furniture. Trotsky and Frida would speak English in front of their spouses, so they could not grasp any of the discussion. Trotsky would sneak his love letters to Frida in the pages of books he would 'loan' to her while he was there.

❦

Diego appeared to most, a nut and a philanderer who would fly into rages from his jealousy when Frida would flirt with men during their marriage which was nothing but stormy for all twenty-four years.

❦

He didn't care if she had a lesbian lover; as it never bothered him. She always came back to him for sex afterward.

❦

He was so hypocritical about his jealousy that in one news-paper supposedly stated that,

"Legend has it that for American women traveling to Mexico,

having sex with Diego was considered as essential as visiting Tenochtitlan."

❦

Diego and Trotsky's wife finally figured out the affair, which by most evidence seems to have ended in July 1937. It was strange, but Diego let Trotsky let them continue to live at La Casa Azul and did not go after him with a gun.

❦

In 1939 there was a huge falling out over politics that caused the Trotskys to finally move out of Diego's home and to a nearby house. Trotsky left a portrait that Frida had painted just for him, "***Between the Curtains***."

❦

Trotsky and Frida stayed friends until Stalin sent an order that Ramon Mercader assassinate Trotsky; Mercader attacked him with an ice ax pick to his head August 20th, 1940 in Trotsky's own home. Trotsky died the next day from his wounds.

❦

Frida was a suspect and held for two days for questioning. Nothing has ever been discovered that survived their love affair. At the end of their tryst, Trotsky had asked Frida for all his old love letters back because he wanted to make sure and burn all of them.

❦

Since this affair had made Diego so angry, Frida seduced Leon Trotsky's secretary, one Ms. Jean van Heijenoort.

⚕

Frida and Diego's friends can remember well how after Trotsky's assassination that Frida would love to make Diego crazy with rage by talking about the affair she had with Trotsky, the Communist. It seemed they lived for heroism and torture.

⚕

When Diego got back from Paris in 1939, he demanded a divorce from Frida. Paulette Goddard was living across the street near Diego's studio. Frida was sure they were having an affair and wondered if they were going to marry. Frida mourned the separation and cut her hair off.

⚕

Frida had huge issues with being by herself in the 1940s. In all her portraits she usually had some item like a doll, monkey, dog, or a parrot in them as if to keep her company. In her house, you would find a mirror in every room, and that included her patio like she needed constant proof that she did exist.

⚕

Frida's health, mental and physical seemed to take a downhill spiral after the divorce. Her pervasive illnesses seemed to exacerbate with her bottle of brandy a day habit, eating a diet of sweets, and chain-smoking.

Because of poor dental hygiene, drinking, and her sweet tooth Frida had several teeth missing, rotted out, or they had turned black. It was the reason that she never smiled in any of her pictures. Because her teeth were rotted, she decided to have two sets of dentures designed, one of them made with studded diamonds and the other made of gold.

In 1940 Frida was racked with pain all down her spine, suffering from kidney infections, developed a nutritional ulcer on her withered foot that had already experienced some gangrenous toes that required removal in 1934, and she had chronic fungal infections on her right hand.

Diego had taken off to San Francisco to avoid the police for the Trotsky assassination as he was under suspicion for a short while. Diego was worried when he heard of Frida's ill health and that she had been jailed for two days and questioned for Trotsky's murder.

Diego sent someone to get Frida and bring her to him, so he could have her hospitalized near him in California. Frida told one of her friends that when she saw Diego, it helped her more than anything else. Frida was ready to marry Diego again, stating that she felt happy.

It still did not prevent Frida from having an affair from her hospital bed with art dealer and collector Heinz Berggruen who was a refugee from Germany.

❧

Heinz is an interesting man indeed as he was a German Jew that got out of Germany before World War II got started.

❧

He took himself to San Francisco and got a job watching over Diego while he was painting a mural there. They had hired Berggruen because he could speak fluent French and would be able to communicate with Diego who could only speak Spanish and French but not even a hint of English. Diego introduced Berggruen to Frida, and the two of them took off to New York to indulge in an affair for one month. After the one month, Frida ran back to Diego, never seeing Berggruen again, and acting as if nothing had ever happened.

❧

When the war was over, Berggruen moved to Paris where he became a leading art dealer for the city for a reign of almost fifty years with his interest mostly in Picassos.

❧

When he returned to Berlin, the city gave him a building for a museum to house his collection of famous paintings and the top floor was his apartment, so he could be near his paintings all the time. He did say that he had felt regret for never owning one of Frida's paintings.

As Berggruen reminisced about his time with Frida, he said it was a time of freedom for Frida because it was during the period while she and Diego were divorced.

Berggruen also explained that during their short affair that he never saw one of her paintings and they had not talked about art. He said after he had met Frida as the woman she was, that was all he needed.

It was only ten days after she left Berggruen that she remarried her Diego on Diego's 54th birthday in San Francisco. They moved back to Mexico and set up their home in Frida's Coyoacan childhood home.

Frida was about to leave Mexico in 1946 to go New York for surgeries with Dr. Wilson when she fell in love with Josep Bartoli, a gorgeous Spanish refugee and a painter like herself. When Frida knew him, he was a vagrant, but fascinated with Frida. For years after their affair, he kept a blouse of Frida's inside an old cigar box to preserve a relic of their love.

Josep was such a quiet person who told only a few of his closest friends. Of course, Frida, on the other hand, revealed to her friend in New York, Ella Wolfe in writing about Josep.

She told Ella that "No one here knows anything, just my sister Cristina and Enrique, my driver and now you of course.

⚜

Frida told Ella if she wanted to talk about Josep in their letters to call him Sonja and asked her to promise once she read the letters to destroy them.

⚜

Josep felt that Frida was the true love of his life. He always said of her that she was loving, romantic and sweet. He thought she was a great artist and very intelligent.

⚜

To Ella, Frida would write that she did indeed love Josep. Josep Bartoli for his entire life kept all forty letters that Frida had written to him. You could recognize the letters were from Frida because of the perfume. Josep could repeat each word, by heart because he had them imprinted in his brain.

⚜

Josep died in 1995, and his family found a chest with his momentos of Frida inside. There were scarves, hair ribbons, sketches, letters, and a small medallion Frida had painted herself and given to him.

⚜

If you turn the medallion over you will find on the back where she wrote:

"For Bartoli, with love. Mara."

Frida used the name as her secret name when she signed her letters to Bartoli. It meant "***wonderful***" in Spanish.

⚜

While Josep and Frida were in Mexico, they made love at Frida's sister Cristina's house, and they kept writing to each other to stay in touch by using a P.O. box in Coyoacan. Frida had told one of her friends that the only reason she was still alive was due to Josep. Josep was the love of her life.

⚜

Her relationship with Diego was more like an obsession, like food for two lost souls. There is a poem that Frida wrote to Diego that Frida's lesbian lover, Teresa Proenza made sure Diego got a few months before he expired.

⚜

It bears witness to all the perverse, raw emotional ties that kept her bound to Diego:

> *"Diego in my urine, Diego in my mouth, in my heart, in my madness, in my sleep..."*

VI

FRIDA WAS ROTTEN TO THE CORE

"I tried to drown my sorrows, but the bastards learned how to swim, and now I am overwhelmed by this decent and good feeling."

— FRIDA KAHLO

In 1946, after having seen multiple Mexican physicians, Frida decided to have major surgery on her spine in New York.

In New York, Dr. Philip Wilson, an orthopedic specialist carried out a spinal fusion by utilizing a bone graft taken from Frida's pelvis and a metal plate.

It seemed after the surgery she had a weird euphoria. She claimed her body was full of vitality.

One will never know if it was the attention of others after the operation itself she received or all the drugs she took for the pain that was causing her euphoria.

In 1950 Frida had an examination that implied that the surgery she had in 1946 in New York might have fused the wrong vertebrae. They opened Frida's back up once again and tried another fusion and this time they used a bone graft from a donor.

Frida's incision became abscessed, and the physicians had to open her wound again. She was in the hospital in Mexico for a year this time.

Frida's wounds did not want to heal because of a fungal infection, and her right leg was looking like gangrene. But in Frida's own crazy Munchausen way, she turned her stay in the hospital into a circus. Diego got a room next door to hers, and the doctors soon realized that when Diego was paying attention to Frida, her pain would disappear.

⚜

Frida's sores oozed, and the doctors would have to drain them. Frida loved the color of the green drainage that came out of the wound. Frida was told NOT to attend the opening of her Mexican art show to be held at the Galeria Arte Contemporaneo.

⚜

Instead, she held a grand entrance for herself where they brought her in on a gurney and placed her in a four-poster bed to lay as a live display. She loved all the attention being on her.

⚜

Diego described Frida as sitting up in the four-poster bed being very quiet but seemingly happy. Diego felt Frida was pleased that so many people had come out to honor her and her paintings.

⚜

It seemed to puzzle Diego that she barely said anything all night, but he felt afterward that she probably had realized she was bidding farewell to life.

⚜

When it came to the surgery that was the most drastic of all operations she had been through in the past; Frida had as many doctors as she had had lovers in her past. So, in August

1953, Frida went back into the hospital to suffer through having her leg cut off at the knee.

※

The nerves had already died, and gangrene was setting in. Doctors told Frida that if the surgery did not take place, she would become septic and die. Frida, with her courage, asked them to proceed with the amputation as soon as they possibly could. It would be her fourteenth surgery in sixteen years.

※

For her entire life, Frida would see a total of thirty surgeries.

※

When Frida was home recovering, sometimes her nurse would call Diego where he was working and let him know Frida was crying uncontrollably and voicing she wanted to die. Diego would stop his painting and rush home to try his best to comfort Frida. When Frida would start to rest peacefully, he would go back to his art and work fast to make up for his lost hours.

※

Diego said there would be some days he was so tired that he would fall asleep in the chair he was sitting on that rested high on the scaffold.

※

Diego finally hired nurses to take care of Frida around the clock. It was expensive and added on with all the other medical costs; it was more than he was making painting murals, so he would have to supplement their income by painting watercolors, sometimes he would paint two a day.

⚜

Frida's spinal column was in such a mess that it indeed was proof that she was "**rotten to the core**."

⚜

In his autobiography, Diego wrote,

> *"After Frida lost her leg, it seemed she went into a deep depression. It was then that she did not even want me to tell her about the love affairs I had been having, and she was losing the will to live."*

⚜

Frida seemed as if she might be rallying around in May 1954. In June she was persistent that she wanted to attend a demonstration and came down with pneumonia. It put her back to bed for another three weeks.

⚜

We must not forget that Frida remained a vain person to the end. She always kept up with her makeup ritual every day no matter what. The Coty Rouge followed by powder on her face, then Talika eye pencil carefully placed on her special unibrow, and always magenta lipstick. She would carefully comb her unibrow and take care of her mustache.

⚜

At last, her professional touch started failing her, and like the surface of her previous canvases, her cosmetics were becoming caked on and smeared. Her features were becoming thickened and coarse, making her look like a boy and distinctly masculine.

⚜

She was almost over pneumonia when one night in July she got up against the doctor's orders and decided to take a bath.

⚜

Within three days Frida was violently ill, and Diego sat by her bed into the wee hours of the morning at Blue House. At four in the morning, she started to complain of severe discomfort. Frida's doctor arrived about daybreak and realized that she had passed away a short time before he had arrived. Cause of death: an embolism to her lungs.

⚜

Even though the doctor said her cause of death was a pulmonary embolism, there was some speculation about what caused her to die. Some feel it may have been a possible suicide.

⚜

Those who pause to wonder about suicide do so because she had tried on several occasions to do away with herself by overdosing or hanging. When she did have livelier moments, it seemed she was always doped up on Demerol; but how did she do it because with all the scabs from all her other injections and scars from all her surgeries no one can find a spot on her skin that you could even insert a needle.

❁

Every sign seemed to point to the facts that Frida's death almost had to be a suicide by overdose. There were too many factors, her diary was among them and support the theory.

❁

Her last words in the diary is a long list of companions and doctors that she is thanking, and then she states that she hopes the leaving is joyful and that she never returns. FRIDA.

❁

In the diary, there is one last self-portrait, and it shows a green face, that looks like a blend of Diego and her features, and under the picture, Frida has printed "*envious one*." The book's very last image is that of a dark winged creature – The Angel of Death.

❁

Diego went in to look at her again, and he said her face was more beautiful and tranquil than he had ever seen it. Just the night before, Frida gave Diego a ring that she had purchased for him as a gift for their twenty-fifth-anniversary that was seventeen days away.

❦

Diego asked her why she was giving it to him so soon and Frida told him that she just had a feeling that she was going to be leaving him soon. Even though she had the feeling she was going to die, plainly she still put up a struggle to live. It just did not make sense to Diego why death came in and surprised her by stealing her breath from her while she slept.

❦

Reports indicate that according to her wishes, they draped her coffin with the Communist flag of Mexico and she lay in state at the Palace of Fine Arts. Some of the government officials raised objections to this display for a revolutionary symbol, and Diego and Frida's friend Dr. Andres Iduarte who was the Director at the Fine Arts Institute lost his job for allowing this to happen.

❦

The newspapers carried the story around the world, and it caused some to raise a fit, so everyone knew of the problem.

❦

Diego said that July 13, 1954, the day Frida died, was the most terrible day of his life. He had lost his beloved Frida forever.

❦

It is said but hard to confirm for 100% certainty that as mourners watched Frida's remains rolling into the vault of the crematory, her mischief had not stopped, and she was still playing nasty tricks on her friends.

જ્જ

When the blast of heat hit as the incinerator doors opened Frida's body that was bejeweled, and her hair so perfectly coiffed felt the high temperature from inside the ovens, and it caused her body to sit bolt upright.

જ્જ

Her hair all ablaze around her face looked like a fiery halo. One onlooker remembered that it seemed to deform her lips and it appeared to break them into a grin at the point the doors closed.

જ્જ

As disgusting as this seems, I do not doubt any of it when you look at the life of Diego and Frida and the way they lived. Diego had a doctor friend that he procured a death certificate from to state Frida's cause of death: "***pulmonary embolism***." Frida's body being quickly cremated so that no one could complete an autopsy.

જ્જ

Olga Campos remembers when she leaned over to kiss Frida's dead body on the cheek before being cremated she could feel Frida's mustache hairs bristling and for a weird moment, their psychologist friend thought Frida was still alive.

When the cremation was complete, and they slid Frida's ashes back out on the cart from the oven, Diego as some witnesses claim, scooped up a handful of the ashes and ate them.

To anyone who knows anything about cremation and the fact that the body is composed mostly of water; more than likely what came out on the cart from the oven would only be very few ashes from Frida's clothes and her bones.

The fires are so hot for cremation that little is left but bone. It makes it hard to believe Diego did pick up the ashes and eat them. There would have been some of the hardware metal pieces that the surgeons had placed in her back during one of the surgeries.

The bones are then taken and ground up to the ash like consistency that you are then called upon later to pick up and place in your urn you have procured for your loved one.

Diego said when the funeral was over he turned over their house in Coyoacan to the Mexican government for a museum for the paintings of Diego that Frida owned. Diego's only stipulations were that there be a corner left for him so that when he did return, he could go to the area where there was the atmosphere to feel Frida's presence.

❧

Once Diego left Coyoacan, he went crazy with the nightclub scene. He hated nightclubs but hated being alone. His only comfort at this point was to rejoin the Communist Party.

❧ VII ❧
SOME CALLED HER A
SURREALIST

"I am happy to be alive, as long as I can paint."

— FRIDA KAHLO

❧

Frida Kahlo's artistic career was admired by many and most
called her a Surrealist, but when you read the definition of a
Surrealist, she does not fit what it defines.

❧

In 1938 Frida felt honored to hold an exhibition at the New
York City Gallery where she sold almost half of her twenty-
five paintings she was showing there.

❧

During the show she locked down two commissions from Clare Boothe Luce, a famous magazine editor that she would have never procured had she not held the show.

❧

In 1939, Frida was invited to have a show in Paris but when she arrived nothing had been set up for the show. Someone that had not even been involved with the show in the beginning hurriedly worked on the event and because of their hard work the show did go on. At this Art Exhibit, she did show some of her paintings and got to know the artists Pablo Picasso and Marcel Duchamp.

❧

The Mexican government commissioned Frida to paint five portraits of famous Mexican women during 1941, but Frida was not able to complete the commission.

A LIFETIME OF FRIDA'S CREATIONS

"I am my own muse, the subject I know best."

— FRIDA KAHLO

❧

Frida created two hundred paintings, sketches and drawings altogether. 143 were paintings, and 55 of them were self-portraits.

❧

Physicians who treated her said that the self-portraits were like reading a medical record about her. She painted what she considered her pathetic life as a child. Then she painted all the pain she suffered from what they thought at the time was polio, then the bus wreck, her miscarriages (who some do not believe were ever miscarriages, and from all research, it is doubtful that they were miscarriages) and through her terrible surgeries later in her life.

HERE ARE A FEW OF HER MOST PROFOUND PAINTINGS

FRIDA AND DIEGO RIVERA (1931)

❧

Frida brought this painting out at the 6th Annual San Francisco Society of Women Artists Exhibition. At the time Frida and Diego were living in San Francisco. She painted this picture two years after she and Diego had married. Frida is holding Diego's hand lightly while he is grasping his painter's palette and his paintbrushes with his other hand. It is a stiff but formal pose maybe hinting to the observer of their tumultuous relationship. This picture hangs at the San Francisco Museum of Modern Art.

HENRY FORD HOSPITAL (1932)

❧

Frida integrated surrealistic and graphic elements in her work in 1932. You will notice in this painting, Frida is naked in a hospital bed, and several items are floating around her but connected to her with a red, string that is veinlike; a snail, flower, fetus, pelvis, and other things. This work is deeply personal to her and tells the story of her second miscarriage.

THE TWO FRIDAS (1939)

⚙️

It is one of Frida's most talked about and famous paintings. It shows two different views of Frida sitting next to each other, and each of them has their hearts exposed to the world. The one Frida being dressed almost entirely in white has a damaged heart, and there are spots of blood on her clothes. The other Frida is wearing bright-colored garments, and her heart is intact. It is the belief that the two Frida's represent an "*unloved*" version of Frida and a "*loved*" version of Frida.

THE BROKEN COLUMN (1944)

⚙️

Frida worked at sharing with the world her physical problems by painting them. This painting showed an almost nude Frida that was split down the center, showing her spine as a shattered decorative column. She is wearing a surgical brace at the same time, and tacks or nails driven into her skin. It was about this time that Frida had been going through several surgeries and had to wear special braces to try to repair her spinal column. Even after this, she would continue through the years to seek other treatments for chronic pain with little to no success.

❧

Frida painted mostly still life pictures when she would have the strength.

HERE IS ANOTHER LIST OF
MORE OF HER PAINTINGS

❦

- Coconuts
- Diego and Frida
- Portrait of Frida's Family
- Diego and I
- Flower of Life (Flame Flower)
- Four Inhabitants of Mexico
- Frida and Diego Rivera
- Fruit of Life
- Fruits of the Earth
- Fulang Chang and I
- Girl with Death Mask
- Frida and the Cesarean Operation
- Henry Ford Hospital (The Flying Bed)
- Itzcuintli Dog with Me
- Landscape
- Living Nature
- Magnolias
- Marxism will give health to the sick

- Me and My Doll
- Me and My Parrots
- Memory the heart
- Moses
- My Birth
- My Dress Hangs There
- My Grandparents My Parents and Me
- My nurse and I
- Pitahayas
- Portrait of a Woman in White
- Portrait of Alejandro Gomez Arias
- Portrait of Alicia Galant
- Portrait of Cristina, My Sister
- Portrait of Diego Rivera
- Portrait of Dona Rosita Morillo
- Portrait of Dr. Leo Eloesser
- Portrait of Eva Frederick
- Portrait of Lucha Maria a girl from Tehuacan
- Portrait of Lupe Marin
- Portrait of Luther Burbank
- Portrait of Marucha Lavin
- Portrait of Miguel n Lira
- Portrait of My Father
- Portrait of Natasha Gelman
- Portrait of Virginia Little Girl
- Roots
- Self Portrait 2
- Self Portrait Along the Border Line Between Mexico and the United States
- Self Portrait as a Tehuana
- Self-portrait dedicated to Dr. Eloesser
- Self-portrait dedicated to Sigmund Firestone
- Self Portrait Dedicated to Leon Trotsky Between the Curtains

- Self Portrait in a Velvet Dress
- Self Portrait in Red and Gold Dress
- Self Portrait the Frame
- Self-portrait Time Flies
- Self Portrait Very Ugly
- Self Portrait with a Monkey
- Self Portrait with a Portrait of Diego on the Breast and Maria between the Eyebrows
- Self Portrait with Bonito
- Self Portrait with Braid
- Self-portrait with Cropped Hair
- Self-portrait with Curly Hair
- Self-portrait with Loose Hair
- Self-portrait with Monkey and Parrot
- Self Portrait with Monkey
- Self Portrait with Monkeys
- Self Portrait with Necklace
- Self Portrait with Necklace of Thorns
- Self Portrait with Small Monkey
- Self Portrait with Stalin
- Self the Chick
- Self Portrait with the Portrait of Doctor Farill
- Self-portrait
- Self Portraitı
- Still Life (Round)
- Still Life with Flag
- Still Life with Parrot and Flag
- Still Life with Parrot
- Still Life with Watermelons
- Still life
- Sun and Life
- The Bride Frightened at Seeing Life Opened
- The Broken Column
- The Bus

- The Deceased Dimas
- The Dream (The Bed)
- The Love Embrace of the Universe the Earth Mexico Myself Diego and Senor Xolotl
- The Mask
- The Suicide of Dorothy Hale
- The Two Fridas
- The Wounded Deer
- The Wounded Table
- Thinking about Death
- Tree of Hope Remain Strong
- Tunas Still Life with Prickly Pear Fruit
- Two Nudes in the Forest the Earth Itself
- Two Women
- Viva la Vida Watermelons
- Weeping Coconuts or Coconut Tears
- What I Saw in the Water
- Without Hope
- Window Display in A Street in Detroit
- Portrait of Mariana Morillo Safa, 1944
- Self Portrait, The Frame, 1938

❧ IX ❧

DIEGO SUFFERS FROM
PENILE CANCER AGAIN

"My painting carries with it the message of pain."

— FRIDA KAHLO

❧

Diego's cancer returned in September of 1955, and he returned to Russia for more treatments at that time.

❧

After losing Frida, Diego did not plan on remarrying anyone ever again, but he met Emma Hurtado who did not care if he could have sex or not. She loved him for who he was, and they kept their marriage secret for about a month. Emma told him she would take care of him while he was sick.

***

Diego felt very lucky as the cobalt treatments, the hospital stays, and everything they did for Diego in Russia did not cost Emma or him a penny.

***

When he first started getting his cobalt treatments again, he was sketching everything that was happening. After he had had several of the treatments, he had gotten so weak; he was not able to even draw a line.

***

He was treated for seven months this time in what was considered to be the best hospital in Moscow, and when they released him, they said he was fit as a fiddle. The doctors there told him if Diego had come to him with his first round of penile cancer, that they would have had him '*cured*' in one month. Before they released him from the hospital, he was given a physical exam and a clean bill of health.

***

He was getting depressed, and the doctors knew that was not a good sign, so they moved him to room in a hotel, so he could watch the parade in Red Square. It did him so much good that he started sketching again.

***

In January he was painting again and with all fury and gusto. In the next six months, he had painted over four hundred pieces of work in Germany, Poland, Czechoslovakia, and Russia. When he got back to Mexico, he went to Acapulco, and painted several oils, watercolors, and drew some sketches.

❧

During the long days that he lay in the hospital, Diego realized that the best part of his life had been loving Frida. However, Diego said that even if he had another chance he doubts he would have behaved any differently than he had the first time around. It seems that a person is the product of what they grow up in and Diego is just Diego.

❧

Diego knew he was not a good person and had no scruples or morals; living only for getting pleasure for himself in any way he could get it. He knew he was not good.

❧

He could figure out the weaknesses of other people and use them to his advantage. Diego said if he loved a woman, that the more he loved her, for some reason, the more he wanted to hurt her. Unfortunately for Frida, she was his victim in this horrible trait. Diego tries to make amends by saying that his life had not been easy either. That everything he had gotten he had to struggle for, and if he got it, he had to fight to keep it. He was not just talking about material goods but the affection of women.

❧

Diego confessed that as he lay in the hospital he tried to add up the meaning of his life and it occurred to him that he had never been "*happy*."

❧

He realized this late in life that the happiest moments in his entire life were when he was painting; all the rest were either sad or boring. When it came to women, if they were not interested in painting, it interrupted my time painting and took time away from something I loved to do while I courted them, so I was not happy if I had to be away from art. The only women I cared about had to love painting, and that was Frida.

❧

After I had painted something and then went back to look at it, I felt a strong sense of aversion for each one of them. The same feeling, I felt toward women who would ask me to make love to them after I had gotten tired of having them around.

❧

November 24th, 1957 Diego succumbed to heart failure and cancer in his studio – San Angel. He had requested that when he passed, he should be cremated, and his ashes mixed with Frida's. Diego's daughters and new wife refused this idea and did not respect his wishes. Instead, they decided that for the nation he should be buried in the "*Rotunda of Famous Men*" there in Mexico City. How sad that they did not honor his last wish.

A MEDICAL DOCTOR'S
PERSPECTIVE ON FRIDA

"I paint flowers, so they will not die."

— FRIDA KAHLO

❦

When most physicians have looked at Frida Kahlo's medical records and tried to explore what caused her pain and suffering all through her life, you find there are differing opinions.

❦

In this chapter, you will find some of them and might agree or disagree, but I feel you will see substantial merit in almost all of them.

They all seem to agree that most of her "*illnesses*" related to neurology.

For example, many of the doctors feel that her neurological problems probably started way before she was even born.

The doctors think she had been born with a congenital anomaly. A nonfusion of her laminae of the spinal arches. Regarding today, Spina Bifida, where the abnormality is due to a defect during the forming in the first month of pregnancy of the neural tube.

It all depends on how severe the defect in its fusion is as to whether the spina bifida will be symptomatic or asymptomatic with it's different urogenital, skeletal and neurological manifestations that include trophic disorders like clubfeet, deformities, motor paresis, and others.

The historical doctors' notes most of the time have ignored the fact she had a malformation or if they did they barely mentioned it. But this was nothing unusual for that time-frame when you had a patient with a congenital defect.

Frida wanted to blame her leg issues on something else that had taken place in her life like trauma or polio. For most of her physicians, they underestimated her spina bifida. What it boiled down to is that most likely all her leg and spine problems through her life were from spina bifida.

❀

Frida became friends with the famous Surgeon Dr. Leo Eloesser in San Francisco in 1930, and he adequately evaluated and noticed Frida's spinal anomaly. The X-rays did show spina bifida, along with the decreased sensitivity he found in the lower part of her extremities was compatible with spina bifida. As she grew and had the numerous operations, it only served to make her right leg and foot problems even worse. Frida tried to hide her leg by wearing long Mexican shirts that were heavily starched.

❀

There are no medical documents on Frida that can be found that speak to her defect, but there are her paintings, one especially '***What I saw in the water***' that illustrates different events in her life.

❀

In this painting, her feet are sticking out of the bathtub, and you can see that between her deformed big toe and the one next to it on her right foot there is a defect that you normally see in congenital neural tube defects.

❀

There is documentation of the displacement of several vertebrae that was probably the cause of her early post-traumatic event, even if it was transient radicular (pain that runs into your lower extremity along a spinal nerve root).

❦

Interestingly, the obvious pain that was worsening in her right leg and spine was found documented several months after what seemed like a full recovery. Together, along with some other factors, it strongly suggests (complex regional pain syndrome type II) or another syndrome that is closely related, RSD (complex regional pain syndrome type I).

❦

The main variance between the two syndromes is a peripheral nerve injury that is the case of complex regional pain syndrome.

❦

If you notice no signs of damage or injury to the peripheral nerve after the accident that has been documented this for sure leans in favor of RSD.

❦

How RSD starts is not understood. It seems that RSD is seen more during mid-life, but it can occur in all ages and that women make up almost 70% of the cases. RSD can develop within a few days or months after someone has had even a minor tissue injury, a bone fracture, some surgical intervention or any prolonged immobilization. Frida had suffered through every one of them.

※

The RSD syndrome symptoms are composed of aching, autonomic dysfunction, dystrophy, atrophy, burning, shooting pain, edema usually of the most distal hand or foot of the extremity that is affected and will sometimes even restrict movement.

※

Doctors have noticed that the pain will usually spread out from the area of the injury, with the potential of affecting both or all four extremities and can be connected with increased sensitivity to pain, ordinarily non-painful stimuli that evokes pain, and pain that is more intense than normally expected and lasts longer than expected.

※

Patients who have RSD are usually anxious and depressed. It seems that Frida felt haunted by all of these and a diagnosis of RSD is probably the right one for her permanent pain that no relief could ever be found.

※

Her pain that could never be relieved seemed to cause her to have many unnecessary surgeries. The primary medical principle − first do no harm − was for sure ignored and caused Frida some severe problems. All the operations that they performed on her leg, foot, and spine made worse her neuropathic pain, that became tremendously severe and devastated her in the last few years of her life.

❧

She suffered from phantom limb pain after they amputated her leg in 1953 and that cannot be forgotten either. One of her sketches from this period in her diary supports that she suffered from this: it showed that cut off below the right knee, the leg is radiating stabbing, shooting pain.

❧

One physician conducted a review of Frida's medical records and studied her artwork and felt that her infertility was because of a condition is known today as Asherman's syndrome.

❧

This syndrome was brought to light in 1894. It seems to occur today as a result when someone has an ordinary but minor surgical procedure such as a dilation and curettage (a technique to clean out the uterus after a miscarriage, childbirth, or an abortion).

❧

Once the basal layer of the uterine endometrium goes under that type of significant damage, the scar tissue will form inside the uterine cavity and start to denote the appearance of Asherman's syndrome. The syndrome can bring on painful cycles, menstrual abnormalities, infertility, and miscarriages.

There are other causes for the syndrome like C-sections, removing fibroid tumors out of the uterus, pelvic irradiation, pelvic surgeries, schistosomiasis, using intrauterine devices, and tuberculosis of the female genitals.

***

Dr. Antelo who was the chief investigator said that Frida's uterine trauma supports a proper diagnosis of the Asherman's syndrome. Especially when she was penetrated by the street-cars handrail when Frida was an adolescent that caused such shock to her uterus. It caused critical injury to her endometrial lining that resulted in some substantial scar formation inside her uterine cavity. That scar formation inside her womb is more than likely the culprit in the continuous pregnancy failures and miscarriages that Frida went through all the time.

***

Frida suffered numerous miscarriages and at least three curative abortions. When one looked at how her paintings revealed images of fertility and reproduction, showing scientifically accurate models of the reproductive organs to accurate portrayals showing the birthing process it helps you understand that she is telling her story of woe.

***

As far as Frida's mental health was concerned, she was diagnosed with minor depression but then suffered at least two significant depressive periods in which she tried to commit suicide during her lifetime.

❦

The fact that she had dissociation and identity problems has led many historians and researchers to feel that Frida suffered from several mental illnesses. From Bipolar Disorder to Post-traumatic Stress Disorder to Dissociative Identity Disorder. Her story seems to fit every disorder and its description.

❦

Dr. Eloesser who had become her dear friend only while she was living in San Francisco also corresponded with Frida when she returned to Mexico. She found she could confide in him and it would be kept just with him and go nowhere else.

❦

Most of their conversations and correspondence had nothing to do with health. Eloesser was ever so caring, wise, and trusted and lived far away. Frida needed someone she could unburden her heart.

❦

Diego was so unfaithful to her, with having affairs with starlets, models, and wealthy tourists. One of his lovers was Louise Nevelson, the American sculptor, and Maria Felix the Mexican film star.

❦

Do not get this author wrong as Frida had her share of men and women lovers, but her husband's roaming and rubbing it in her face caused her so much pain. The most profound pain came when he had an affair with her sister, Cristina.

❦

Frida told Dr. Eloesser that he had no idea how her husband made her suffer. Life with Diego got to where it was intolerable, so in 1939, they filed for divorce.

❦

Because she was not with the man she loved every day, Frida went into a deep but dark emotional state and started drinking more than she ever had before.

❦

It was during this time she painted herself in a self-portrait wearing a necklace of thorns, while her heart was exposed and dripping blood in another portrait.

❦

Frida became very ill; the Mexican physicians placed her in traction and told her she needed more surgery. In only three months she had lost fifteen pounds.

❦

Diego was in San Francisco painting a mural that he had been commissioned to commemorate the Golden Gate Exhibition. Diego consulted Dr. Eloesser. Diego was worried about Frida, she was so far away and so ill, so Diego asked Dr. Eloesser for his advice.

❧

Dr. Eloesser called Frida and asked her to come to San Francisco and let him care for her there in his hospital. He wrote her a letter explaining to her what he thought was the cause of why she was suffering all the time.

❧

He went on to tell her that Diego did love her very much and that you, Frida know you love him. Frida, you know that Diego will never be monogamous, and it is best to accept him like he is and to turn your head and channel all your energy into your work the best you can. But, I feel it is best that you remarry Diego. Dr. Eloesser closed the letter by telling Frida to reflect on what he had told her to make a decision.

❧

In the meantime, Dr. Elosesser talked to Diego and told him that remarrying Frida would be best for her health. Diego told one of his assistants that he felt Frida needed him.

❧

He went on to tell his assistant that to reconcile with Frida would be best for him as well. Diego felt that living away from Frida had hurt both of them.

❧

In September 1940, Frida flew to Diego in San Francisco, and Dr. Eloesser admitted her to St. Luke's so she could rest, and he could make sure she got dried out from liquor while he watched her health continue to improve.

⚜

When Diego would visit Frida's room, they would talk about getting back together. Before they could decide on anything, Frida took off to New York to meet up with the owner of a gallery, and it so happened while she was there she had a whirlwind fling with the young German lover of art, Heinz Berggruen.

⚜

In late November, Frida was still in New York and had finally made up her mind to marry Diego again. She told Diego that when they married again it would have to be only a marriage of souls and they would not have any physical intimacy.

⚜

Diego said that he was so glad to get Frida back that he agreed to everything. Frida went back to San Francisco and lived in Eloesser's house until she and Diego had a brief wedding ceremony in the city courtroom.

❧ XI ❧
FINAL WORDS

❦

While writing this book and researching Frida and Diego, it leads one to believe that the two of them never grew up. They both wanted their way all the time, no matter what. They both had a vindictive spirit about them it seemed.

❦

The mere fact that Frida had to fill Diego's bathtub with children's toys as she bathed him each time is no way '***normal***' in most books.

❦

It seems that Frida had a narcissistic personality as she

thought a lot of herself and suffered from Munchausen syndrome. It does make one wonder how in the world these two people ever came together as husband and wife. What was the attraction for the two of them to desire joining their lives?

❦

It is hard to imagine all the infidelities during their marriage. Diego was a declared Atheist, and even though Frida was born into a Catholic – Lutheran family, it is assumed that she may have possibly been an Atheist at the time of her death. Maybe being an Atheist, it is okay to have numerous lovers.

❦

It's not sure that Frida would have ever been famous had she not caused her suffering and all to gain the attention of others. Especially the attention of Diego.

❦

While some of the doctors want to give her an excuse for her miscarriages, it is harder after researching to believe that they were real miscarriages. It felt like she terminated them in some fashion. It is hard to think that Frida ever wanted a child. There would be no attention lavished upon her, and it is doubtful she could live with that.

❦

Maybe this judgment of Frida is incorrect, after all, this is only based on research, and we have not walked in her shoes.

It appears that she never had any real happiness in her life, but she tried for 47 years on this earth to find happiness and pursued it relentlessly the best she knew how. It seems that happiness continued to elude her for her entire life.

❧ XII ❧
FRIDA'S WEAKNESSES

❦

Munchausen Syndrome – her constant need for attention, so she always tried to be sick to draw that attention to herself.

❦

Frida's infidelities seemed to be used to try and get even with Diego.

❦

Frida's insecurities about her own body caused her to give herself away to men more freely.

❦

If Frida had been appropriately diagnosed when she was younger, her life might have been entirely different.

❦

If Frida had not had a unibrow, waxed her upper lip, and shaved under her arms, she may have appeared more feminine than she did, and it may have given her more self-confidence. She never gave herself a chance because she felt it was her job to be the boy in the family.

❧ XIII ❧
FRIDA'S STRENGTHS

❦

She was a strong person who never gave up once she started something. Never let handicaps make you think that you cannot succeed in life, there is always something you can do to overcome almost all handicaps if you want to succeed in life because it is there for the taking!

❦

For all that she had been through in life, she forged on and became a success with her paintings. (Unfortunately, her paintings were worth much more after she had died than when she was alive.) If one person does not appreciate what you are doing, do not count yourself a failure, one person's opinion does not count you down and out. The next person may have the impression that you have what it takes to be a success!

※

She was careful to take advantage of all the famous people she met and position herself so that she could use them in the future to further her goals in her life. Remember to never burn any bridges behind you for you never know when you may have to walk back across that bridge again in your future.

❧ XIV ❧
RECOMMENDED READS

૭૪૭

- A Biography of Frida Kahlo by Hayden Herrera 4.5/5 rating
- Frida Kahlo: Life and Work by Helga Prignitz-Poda 4.3/5 rating
- Frida Kahlo at Home by Suzanne Barbezat 4.2/5 rating

YOUR FREE EBOOK!

As a way of saying thank you for reading our book, we're offering you a free copy of the below eBook.

Happy Reading!